# A short book about reaching Your goals

Editor and Translator: Emelie Johansson

Publisher: BoD – Books on Demand, Stockholm, Sverige
Printer: BoD – Books on Demand, Norderstedt, Tyskland

ISBN: 978-91-7699-743-7

# Contents

# Preface

Having a goal, and even more so reaching your goal, is a fascinating and almost addictive process. With the right circumstances it will guide you to personal growth and important experiences. It demands you to find and explore your inner drive. And in the best of worlds, you learn to understand it.

I believe every human has felt it at one point or another in their life. The inner drive is like a fiery sensation placed just below the chest. It makes your blood boil and your heart beat faster. The inner drive is like an engine to get things done. The source of your inner drive is your gasoline. It plays a role in feelings of inspiration, creativity and courage. The book talks about the Serbo-Croatian attitude of sorts called "Inat".
I think "inat" describes something that in Swedish is called "jävlar anamma". It is an expression for boldness, fighting spirit, force, temper. To possess "jävlar anamma" is to be passionate about something and have ambition – the mentality that you can do just about anything to ensue your goal.

Finding your inner drive and defining its source is an essential part of understanding yourself and achieve personal growth. Feelings connected to the inner drive is a great help in many aspects of life. It's what gets you places. I believe, for many people childhood sets the foundation for developing this inner drive.

For me, growing up an underdog as the youngest girl of three siblings with a single mother in the suburbs, gave me a foundation of gratitude but also incredible power. I took nothing for granted and no one expected anything from me. And this made me want to prove everything. I could do just as good, or even better, than the boys from the nicer areas. I was always thankful for everything I had and the possibilities I could enjoy, and I would let nothing slip.

I'm an underdog from which no one expects anything, but with the possibilities to do almost anything. This is the source of my inner drive. It pushes me forward in life, saying yes whenever I'm met with a challenge. My inner drive makes me face my fears, because I *can* and because I have something to prove. It has taken me through university with straight A's, to the muay thai boxing ring, to leadership positions at a young age and lecturing even though I'm a highly anxious person.

I was asked to translate and edit this book by my friend Veselko. I don't know the source of his inner drive yet, it's a story still untold. However, I've seen proof of his inner drive many times and I know that when he claims to have reflected upon and figured something out regarding how to reach your goal, he really has. He is a stubborn person who will never give up, nor take no for an answer if he believes he has a good idea. Whether it is developing the best oatmeal recipe, opening up his own gym or writing and publishing his own book. He is going to get there.

Emelie Johansson
Translator and Editor

Veselko Lakobrija
Author

# Do you have what it takes to reach your goal?

To endeavor reaching a goal is to set out on a journey, regardless of what kind of goal you are attempting. You might want to become an athlete, artist, entrepreneur, musician or whatever else. To reach your own personal goal gives you more than just the right to brag. It gives fulfillment and a sense of purpose in life, especially if the goal attempted is greater than you. Furthermore, the journey is so humbling that no one who has reached their goal would brag about it. These people let the outcome speak.
An old Latin saying goes: "Acta, non verba" or "Actions, not words".

The journey comes with its own demands, which has to be fulfilled in any kind of way. And the methods of fulfilling these demands should be specifically suiting to you if you are to be successful on the journey towards the goal. It requires two attributes:

Discipline is one. It is the second attribute (no, I haven't forgotten the first). Discipline can be developed, increased and improved. This essentially means that it is okay to be completely undisciplined at current. It can be resolved.

When defining discipline it is synonymous with maintaining order and following routine. It could further denote a personal trait. A disciplined person fulfills their commitments and acts according to their notion of what would be the best thing to do, even if such actions entails discomfort in the short term. This trait is widely considered a virtue. *(WIKIPEDIA)*

So how is discipline developed? It is rather simple, however not always easy…

One way is to make sure the first thing you do in the morning is to not hit the snooze button but get up, turn the alarm off, and then make the bed. Or simply do the dishes as soon as need arises. Don't let any of the simplest chores wait. These are two examples of starting and then continuing your day in a productive manner. And these actions are heavily dependent on the first attribute.

Personally, the first thing I do in the morning is get up and do 15 burpees with push-ups. Sometimes I switch it to 5 minutes of skipping rope. The reason for this routine is purely biological. Both activities release adrenaline, and to my knowledge no person can sleep with adrenaline surge in their blood stream. This wakes me up, and builds on my discipline.

# Have a goal or destination

A wise man once said:
"Everything is a harbor to a ship without a destination".

Think, fantasize, dream about your goal or do whatever it takes for you to find your goal. Search inwards to explore whatever sparks your joy or get inspired by others. As you find your destination out, write it down on a piece of paper. Cherish this piece of paper as this will both work as a guide towards what you need to do to reach your goal, and remind you of it as distractions occur on the way there.

Make sure that you care about the goal that you set out to achieve. The goal needs to and should be important and meaningful to you. There has to be meaning when the going gets rough, regardless of what the goal consists of. Why else would you accept having a tougher existence on a daily basis, with less free time, perhaps less money, or even being unable to put food on the table for periods of time?
You need to be committed to your goal to endure on the journey, and yes, it is a rough journey that you embark on. So, how do you define and write your goal or destination down? Your goal should be:

- Specific - if your goal is vague, how will you know that you´ve reached your destination?
- Written down - remind yourself to keep on track when weather gets cloudy (it will get stormy).
- Challenging - growth gives meaning to the process.
- Credible or Realistic - nothing beats you down as much as never experiencing any kind of success.
- Measurable - how will you know how far you have gotten? Every step counts, so make sure they are countable.

- Have a deadline - it seems to be a human trait to work better under a certain amount of pressure.

Even easier to remember is SMART. The acronym, widely mentioned in management literature, stands for:

Specific
Measurable
Achievable
Realistic
Timely

Keep this in mind as you determine and define your goal, as these criteria to help you focus your efforts and in the long run help you reach your destination.

Consider following when you define your goal:

1. What do you want?
   Write down exactly what you want (and don't begin this with writing down what you don't want) that you can achieve yourself - not what you want someone else to do for you. Be specific. Writing down you wish for more money is not specific, however writing down you want to earn 5000 Euros, Dollars or whatever the currency more a month is very specific, and countable.

2. What does it mean for you to reach this goal?
   This is where you envision what your efforts could provide you with. Is it worth the struggle?

3. How do you know when you've reached it?
   Describe what you will see, hear and feel when you have reached it.

4. When do you want it?
   This is your deadline. This is where you put down the end date.

5. What stops you from already having it?
   This shows you what obstacles you need to overcome, and also reveals what you need to do to get over them.

6. How will the goal affect other parts of your life?
   You will have positive as well as negative effects to take a stand on. The negative effects come with sacrifices and waivers of different kinds. You might need to give up pizza, stop playing computer games, stop drinking alcohol or change the people you surround yourself with... just to mention a few.

7. What do you have today to help you reach your goal?
   What resources, knowledge, contacts and competences do you already possess?

8. What do you need to be able to reach your goal?
   A positive attitude always helps. But it is even better when you add (more) knowledge. Read books on the subject, take a class or course, talk to people involved in the area and build a network of contacts with people who has already pursued a similar journey.
   "Knowledge is power" is not a full adage so here it is as it needs to be:
   "Applied knowledge is power."

9. What is the easiest way to get there?
   Which is the absolutely first step you need to take? Which steps can you take today? Are there several ways to do it, and which way is more likely to be successful? Which is the

fastest way, and is there a conflict between time, efficiency and quality?
Last but not least, which step is the easiest to take?
Begin there.

I came to think of Simon Sinek here and his "Start with why". Simon's book, or YouTube videos (however I recommend a book), has nothing to do with reaching your goal but it is about inspirational leadership. It is rather easy to implement this way of thinking in your goal reaching journey. Simons thoughts on defining and communicating your "why" is a never ending source of inspiration.

# **Focus**

Now that you have defined and written down your goal, you need to make sure to keep focused during the process. Building and maintaining focus is not that complicated, you just need to:

- Have powerful reasons
  the more powerful reasons, the more motivation to reach your goal. The more motivation, the easier it is to stay focused. Make sure the reason "why" is yours. If it is not - make it yours!

- Visualize
  Athletes see themselves winning long before the race has even started. Visualize how it would feel to reach your goal. How people will talk about you*. The more detailed the vision, the more powerful it will be. It will be like a magnet pulling you towards your goal.

- Confirm your sub-goals
  Write down your sub-goals or milestones, however small they seem to be. Confirm them and celebrate them.

- Measure your sub-goals
  If it can't be measured, it can't be improved. If it cannot be improved it will eventually stagnate, and stagnation does not lead forward.

- Look for support from others
  Surround yourself with people who support and challenge you. Chose a person to present your progress to, so that you have someone other than yourself to keep you on track.

*This one is a bit tricky, mostly because you shouldn't really care about what others think, but for some it gives a certain amount of motivation.*
Here are some keys to why and how:

1. People who don't care - these you will only find if you ask for people's opinions;
2. People who are positive towards your project;
3. People who are negative towards your project;

As you reach your goal the first group, if you find them, will still not care at all. The other group will share your joy. The third group, now this is the one you should really listen to. But don't change your behavior, and don't let them affect your decision making. That is not why you should be listening to them. The reason is for you to use these people and their negative words as fuel for your drive forward on your journey towards your goal. It´s not only tricky but quite risky too, but it does add energy to your struggle.

In Serbo-Croatian there is a word "inat". "Just because" is the closest to a translation that I can find. I'm not sure if it is a matter of attitude, upbringing, a way of thought or part of the culture. But it is powerful. Here's one example how it works: A negative person tells you: "It is too hard, you will fail". Then you go: "Oh, you think?" with a gentle smile and then you get to work. When you accomplished what you set out to do, ask this negative person just one question: "Please, remind me... What was it you told me just before I started this journey?" If you care enough to listen to their answer, be prepared for some excuses. Most of them are excuses towards your success itself, however that is possible.

While on the subject on "inat" there is one more thing. Some of these negative people may start to think "Wait a minute... I doubted this person, even made fun of him/her and look at them now. Why don't I try something like this?"

If you are lucky this person may even come to you in search of advice, and here you have a choice:
- Be humble and teach how;
- Be a negative a\*\*hole and walk away;

Whichever way you choose to act. I prefer the first one.

And if this person came back to you or not does not affect you. It makes no difference what so ever. The point is, embarking and succeeding on your journey might have bigger winnings than the personal growth of you - you might inspire others, even turn the negative frowns upside down!
Well done.

However, if you are not sure you can stay unaffected by others' negativity, keep away from these people as described further on in this book.

*"And if you lose your focus?"*
Emelie asked me this and the question surprised me, as I don't think about this anymore. I just go, or even live with it.
However, if you lose your focus and find yourself lost, it is easily managed - you wrote a note in the beginning of this process, remember?
Read it.
Read it every time you find yourself losing your focus. This is why you should always write your goal down. Not because you will forget what it is, but it helps you remember the feeling you had when you wrote it down.

Backlashes will happen. I expect backlashes, however I do not welcome them. Backlashes fills a very important purpose, they ensure that you really want to reach this goal and is not just doing it in lack of something better to do. Backlashes separates the chaff from the wheat.

She also mentioned failures. Well... there are no failures in life. Either you reach your goal or you learn something new. I can't understand why people would consider new knowledge a failure. In this sense, failure could even be considered a gift.

> *"Success is stumbling from failure to failure*
> *with no loss of enthusiasm"*
> *Winston Churchill*

> *"You never fail until you stop trying."*
> *Albert Einstein*

Don't forget that you can achieve whatever you want, but not everything you want.

Last but not least - Celebrate!
Never forget to celebrate and reward yourself for your achievements, even the smallest ones, and anyone else who helped you made them happen. This will remind you where you came from and where you are today. It will motivate you to reach the next milestone or sub-goal.

During celebration, reflect upon:
- What was the goal or sub-goal that I wished to achieve?
- What worked well and how could it be even better?
- What didn't work well and how can that be improved or even rejected?

# Fear

It is natural to experience fear as you begin a journey to reach a highly set goal. This is unknown territory you find yourself in so the feeling is not unexpected. The greater the fear, the more valuable and credible is the goal that you set for yourself.
If you don't experience fear, the journey is not worth the effort and time put to it. And the goal even less so.

So how do you handle fear?
You need to start by admitting that the fear is real and the feelings are there. It is okay to be scared, after all you have no idea of what you can anticipate and what you will face during the journey. You can make a guess, but even if the guess would turn out to be right it is still just a guess. Admittedly a successful one, but not a fact nor knowledge.

Next, you need to accept those feelings and make friends with them. Fear will keep you sharp and focused. Just ensure that they will not get in your way, or take over.
Fear might take over in one of the following ways, or even both at the same time:

- Fear steps in front of you, looks you in the eyes and says "Do something, you coward"
- Fear sits on your shoulder and whispers: "You don't have what it takes, you will never make it. You are going to fail."

At this point you need to answer the question of who is calling the shots. Is it me or is it my fears?

If you decide it's your fears… well good luck with that and the rest of your life.

If you decide to be in charge, be prepared to roll up your sleeves and get to work. This will be a fight against fear, and you need to persist until fear has given up. Remind yourself of why you want to reach your specified goal. Imagine how good it will feel as you get there. Go back to your notes and your visions, search for your motivation and try to turn the negative thoughts around by focusing on the positive feelings attached to your goal.

Talk about your fears with your friends, family, colleagues and others who have already headed out on a journey like your own. It is important to reflect upon your feelings together with someone else, who has an outsider's perspective. If not to give advice, so at least to listen. Saying things out loud can actually make the bad feelings go away, as it lets you hear what you otherwise just think and feel. When said out loud, you might even experience these thoughts as rather silly - and they are easier to drop.

Do not seek support in people who has expressed doubts regarding you or your goal. Watch yourself from the people who told you that it is ridiculous, crazy or even dangerous to head out on your journey. Watch yourself from them, even more than you should watch yourself from your own feelings of fear. Their negativity will spread easily and with high pace. And worst of all, this negativity will enhance fear.

Alternatively, you could fight fear and negativity with some "inat" attitude as described earlier. And remember, that the right thing is almost always the most difficult one.
Your success is the best, maybe even the only, weapon that you have against these people. Just wait and see where they are, what they do and hear them talk after you reach your goal. Likely is that they are staying in the exact same spot.

Negativity and fear never has, it does not nor will it ever take you forward.

## A life without fear

Once upon a time, there was a young warrior. His teacher told him that he had to battle with fear.
But he didn't want to do that. It seemed too aggressive, it was scary. It seemed unfriendly.
But then the teacher told him that he had to do it and gave him the instructions for the battle.

And then the day arrived.
The student warrior, stood on one side and fear, stood on the other side.
The warrior was feeling very small and fear was looking big and wrathful.
They both had their weapons.

The young warrior roused himself and went toward fear, prostrated three times and asked:
"May I have permission to go into battle with you?"
And Fear said:
"Thank you for showing me so much respect that you ask permission."

Then the young warrior said: "How can I defeat you?"
And fear replied:
"My weapons are that I talk fast, and I get very close to your face.
And then you get completely unnerved, and you do whatever I say.
If you don´t do what I tell you, I have no power. You can listen to me and you can have respect for me, you can be convinced by me.
But if you don´t do what I say I have no power…"

And in that way the student warrior learned how to defeat fear.

Buddhist story found on "Dare to do" YouTube channel

## Loneliness

The goal you set up for yourself is yours. And the journey is yours to make. How many people can you expect to be able to and even want to be part of it, completely on your terms? Yes you read it correctly, your journey - your terms. Others' terms or opinions are not applicable here.

Yes, it is just you. No one can experience it but you. No friends, family, brothers, sisters, parents can fully grasp what you are going through. Only you decide the turns and potential detours of this journey, and only you can reach your destination. Only you will or will not compromise during this time. Alone.

Scary? Yes, it is. I know. Please return to the previous chapter to reflect on this, or use my favorite strategy: "inat". Smile and say it out loud: "These people want to see me fail, and boy, will they see some failures!".

If you learn to trust your intuition, or gut feeling, this loneliness can be a source for your motivation and persistence.
When I talk about loneliness I don't talk about living your life alone, but you will be forced to spend a lot of time alone and in silence during the journey, for thinking.

Make sure you have access to a small room, basement, a grove or whatever little place where you are completely alone and with as little visual external influence as possible. No, you don't need a fancy laboratory environment to exercise active thinking and reflecting.

This is to give you opportunity to go through, reflect, and analyze your steps up to this point... to just think.

You will for instance realize that some steps of your journey were completely wrong. But as long as you learn from it, it was not a failure. Leave the slip behind, bring the knowledge it provided with you and carry on.

Or, another step was just right and you took it a few times. Maybe these activities should be streamlined? Make sure it is faster and easier done.

# Development

When it comes to development it is as personal as the rest of the journey. You will experience, discover and learn incredibly much during this journey that will be of value for your personal growth. If you don't learn or grow, you are heading towards the wrong destination.
A lack of the sense of development is the only acceptable reason to quit the journey, as then it has no value and nothing to offer you.

If you experience this, you need to return to the drawing board and envision a new goal. Start to aim higher, probably a lot higher.
Like my mother used to tell me:

*"If you aim too high and you miss boy, there's no problem. But if you aim too low and you hit, then you and me are going to have a serious talk. If you aim to low and miss, don't even bother coming home".*

I had that talk with her three times - the first, the only and the last time.
My mother is a tough woman. These three times were when I was a six year old boy training karate. I know, a ridiculous martial art. I was confused about learning how to fight without actually hitting an opponent.
But karate built discipline. With my 120 cm and 25 kg, I was the second smallest and next to youngest in the group. There was a five year old who was a head shorter than me. The rest of the group was ten or above.
After a few weeks training and too many reprimands about not really hitting physically, I defeated the five year old. Overjoyed, I ran home to my mother to share the news. My mother

responded: "When you defeat that boy", and referring to the largest boy in the group, "then come to me to brag".
I continued to hit for real. "If you are learning how to fight, you should fight for real" was my perspective. My trainer moved me to the full contact group. Youngest, smallest and with least experience. How much beating I got... It hurt but I didn't care - I could learn to fight for real in this group.

At my first contest, the summer before first grade, after 8 months of training, I won third place and I was so angry with myself. After talking to my trainer and my parents I trained at any hour of the day. On next contest, I was 8 years old competing with boys 13-15 years old.
On the competition day my mother told me: "If you want to brag about your skills, you need to defeat that boy". A 14 year old. I thought: "Ok, I'm really going to brag!". The drive to be able to brag, and to impress my mother, took me to the final, against that 14 year old.

I had nothing to give against this boy, and in pure rage I hit him straight in the throat to the Adam's apple. He fell to the floor covering his throat. I continued to kick and hit him until both of our trainers pulled us apart and tried to help him.
I had no idea how dangerous this blow could be, but he was taken away in an ambulance. And I was disqualified from competing for five years.

But I "won" the competition and bragged to my mother, and she responded:
"There is just one thing worse than a bad looser, and that is a bad winner. You can't be a bad winner".
My dad filled in with: "And on top of all that, you can't compete for five years. So what did you win?"

Since that day I'm quiet as a grave and I let my actions do the talking, I have no desire to brag.

## The lacking attribute

Now it's time to go back to the first, and the most important attribute, to complete this journey:

## Willpower

Without it, we as humans can't do anything. In the most extreme, not even live our lives.
Do you remember the feeling of purpose?

According to definition, will is the mental capacity that means exercising a conscious control over thinking and handling.
Besides the disagreement regarding how to define will, there is also disagreement on how people absorb knowledge regarding their own attitudes of will.

"The little engine that could" is a children's story which is certainly applicable here. If you haven't read it, or had it read to you from your parents, read it now. It is not too late.
Shortly, it tells the story of a train who needs to cross a hill or a mountain, not sure.
It was a long time since I was a kid. This train couldn't do it on its own and it received help from the smallest little locomotive, who succeeded its task thanks to believing it could!

When it comes to willpower the rule is as easy as simple:


"Wherever is a will, there is way"

I would like to finish this chapter with two quotes from American Football coach Vince Lombardi:

*"A man can be as great as he wants to be. If you believe in yourself and have the courage, the determination, the dedication, the competitive drive, and if you are willing to sacrifice the little things in life and pay the price for the things that are worthwhile, it can be done.*
*Once a man has made a commitment ... he puts the greatest strength in the world behind him. It's something we call heart power. Once a man has made this commitment, nothing will stop him short of success."*

*"The difference between a successful person and others is not a lack of strength, nor a lack of knowledge, but rather a lack of will."*

## Epilogue

By now, you've probably started thinking:
- Is this daily work?
- Is it hard?
- What will it demand of me?
- And how much of it?

These worries are all based on fears of the unknown and overcoming them is your first ground-breaking step. Challenge your fears and concerns and by doing so, defeat them.

One last tip:
When you start your journey, know that you are in it for the long run. Quitting is not an option now.
Why, you ask?

Well... whatever it is you start and not complete, or if you make a resolution that you don't keep, you are forming a habit of failure. So when you start, see it through – even if the heavens above you fall down.

What I need to tell you now is somewhat deterrent. I'm not doing it to make you hesitate, decide for an easier destination, or even worse give up. Don't!
I'm writing this to give you a warning, so that you are prepared. Here we go:

Even if you decide to implement these rules, if you can call them rules, and even if you do it by the book and with military precision. Even if you breathe, eat and live everything that this book mentions, I (or anyone else) cannot guarantee that you will actually end up reaching your goal.

It´s also about having a just a slight touch of good luck on your side.

The strategies in this book are your greatest support. And if they fail, I'm sorry for that. I'm also sorry for not knowing how to keep these intact throughout the entire journey. I don´t know because they never failed me so I never got a lesson. That is the real struggle.

Dear reader, see you on the other side of the finish line.

I wish you the best of luck. You will need it.
After all:

*Audentes Fortuna Iuvat*

*Veselko Lakobrija*